THE STORY OF THE OLYMPICS

First published in Great Britain in 2011
by Orion Children's Books
a division of the Orion Publishing Group Ltd
Orion House, 5 Upper St Martin's Lane, London WC2H 9EA
An Hachette UK Company

The Orion Publishing Group's policy is to use papers
that are natural, renewable and recyclable products
and made from wood grown in sustainable forests.
The logging and manufacturing processes are expected
to conform to the environmental regulations
of the country of origin.

A catalogue record for this book is available from the British Library

Printed in China

www.orionbooks.co.uk

"Sport has the power to change the world.
It has the power to unite in a way that little else does.
It speaks to youth in a language they understand.
Sport can create hope where once there was only
despair. It is more powerful than governments in
breaking down racial barriers. It laughs in
the face of all types of discrimination."

Nelson Mandela

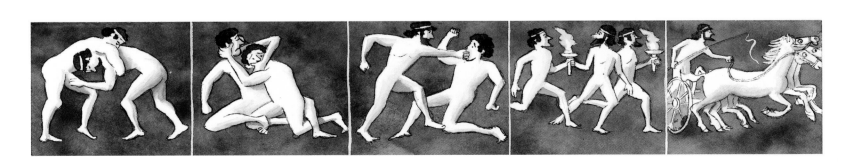

How old are you?

Two and a half Olympiads.

THE OLYMPIAD AND THE OLYMPIC TRUCE

In ancient times the land of Greece was made up of many small kingdoms, which constantly fought among themselves. But every four years they agreed to put aside their differences and send their best athletes to compete with each other in games held at a place named Olympia. The four-year period between the start of one games and the next became known as an Olympiad. It was even used to measure time.

The games at Olympia were not just a sporting event. They were also a religious festival dedicated to Zeus, the king of the Greek gods. After 293 Olympiads, Christianity became the state religion of Rome and the Emperor put a stop to the Games.

Let's stop the war for a bit and run some races instead.

OK

These Games are unchristian.

1600	1766	668TH OLYMPIAD 1896	1900	1916
FIRST COTSWOLD OLIMPICKS	REDISCOVERY OF ANCIENT OLYMPIA	FIRST GAMES OF THE MODERN ERA	FIRST WOMEN COMPETE	WORLD WAR ONE • NO GAMES

146 | AD | 67 | 393 | 426

ROMANS ARRIVE AND TAKE OVER THE GAMES

EMPEROR NERO COMPETES IN CHARIOT

ROMAN EMPEROR THEODOSIUS BANS THE GAMES AS PAGAN CULT.

TEMPLE OF ZEUS BURNT TO THE GROUND.

> It's more important in life to compete than to triumph. To have fought well is the main thing, not to have won.

Pierre de Coubertin

THE OLYMPIC IDEAL

When Baron Pierre de Coubertin restarted the Olympic Games just over a hundred years ago, he hoped the meeting of athletes from all over the world would lead to peace and better understanding between nations. He also hoped that the athletes would take part for the joy of sport and not just for money or fame.

Today athletes from almost every nation compete to be the best in their chosen sport. It doesn't matter what country they come from. People in every part of the world can take pleasure in watching them do the best they can.

1924 | 1928 | 1936 | 1940/44

FIRST WINTER OLYMPICS

FIRST WOMEN'S TRACK & FIELD EVENTS

FIRST TORCH RELAY FROM OLYMPIA

WORLD WAR TWO · NO GAMES

1960 FIRST PARALYMPICS
1968 FIRST SPECIAL OLYMPICS
2010 FIRST YOUTH OLYMPICS

DID HERACLES START THE OLYMPICS?

The Greek myths tell us how mighty Heracles cleaned the stinky Augean stables by damming the river Alpheus so it flowed through them. Afterwards he cleared all the rocks from the plain beside the river, known as the Altis, and held the first Olympic Games there in honour of his father, Zeus.

A SLIGHTLY MORE LIKELY STORY

King Iphitos of Elis got so fed up with all the different Greek states fighting each other that he went to see the Delphic Oracle, who could see into the future. She told him to hold some games at Olympia.

THE OLYMPIC TRUCE

Iphitos sent heralds to every state to announce a truce so athletes and spectators could travel to the Games without fear of attack.

THE OLYMPIC PROCESSION

The Games were to be held every four years after the harvest. The first took place in 776 BC. Two days before they began, officials, athletes and trainers set out on the two-day walk from Elis to Olympia.

In the 720BC Olympics, Orsippos' shorts fell down and tripped him up during a race.

To stop this happening again, the judges told the athletes to take their shorts off.

And, for the next thousand years, Olympic competitors wore no clothes at all.

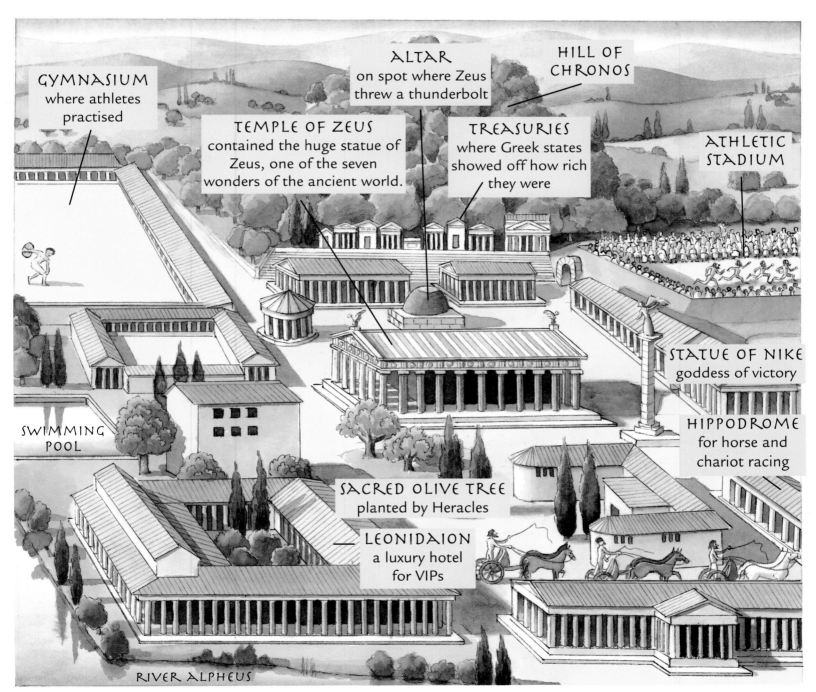

GYMNASIUM
where athletes practised

ALTAR
on spot where Zeus threw a thunderbolt

HILL OF CHRONOS

TEMPLE OF ZEUS
contained the huge statue of Zeus, one of the seven wonders of the ancient world.

TREASURIES
where Greek states showed off how rich they were

ATHLETIC STADIUM

STATUE OF NIKE
goddess of victory

HIPPODROME
for horse and chariot racing

SWIMMING POOL

SACRED OLIVE TREE
planted by Heracles

LEONIDAION
a luxury hotel for VIPs

RIVER ALPHEUS

THE SITE OF THE ORIGINAL OLYMPIC GAMES

In time the sports complex spread over the Altis plain at Olympia. The Games were an important religious festival dedicated to the god Zeus. The Greek states competed to build temples and other fine buildings.

THE MARATHON

Amazingly, today's great closing event was never a part of the Ancient Games.

The legend goes that when the Persian army landed at Marathon in 490 BC an Athenian named Pheidippides ran 150 miles to Sparta to get help. He then ran back to Marathon to find the Athenians had already beaten the Persians, so he raced to Athens and just managed to gasp news of the victory before croaking.

It's 25 miles from Marathon to Athens. Pierre and the others thought it would be great to end the 1896 Games with a race over that distance.

Edwin Flack of Australia was a great athlete but he failed to finish the first Marathon in Athens despite being accompanied by a butler on a bicycle.

FIRST MARATHON CHAMPION

Spiridon Louis

Spiridon was a water-carrier from Athens. The home crowd were ecstatic when he entered the stadium in first place. The king said he could have any prize he wanted. He asked for a new water cart. To 'do a Louis' in Greek still means to run very fast.

KLUTZ ALERT!
The 54-year marathon

Shizo Kanaguri seemed to vanish during the 1912 race. In fact he'd fallen asleep beside the road. In 1966 he returned to Stockholm to finish the course.

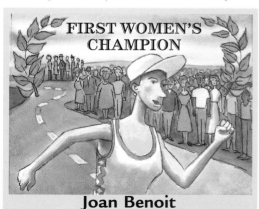

FIRST WOMEN'S CHAMPION

Joan Benoit

The first women's marathon was not introduced until 1984! It was won by Joan, from Maine, USA, wearing her trademark painter's hat.

In 2004 the race was once again run from Marathon to Athens. It was sadly spoilt when a spectator pushed the leader, de Lima of Brazil, off the course.

THE WACKY MARATHON

With competitors nearly dying from exhaustion, taking shortcuts and disappearing, the early marathons often seem more like the Wacky Races than an Olympic event. But none was wackier than the St Louis Marathon of 1904.

START

FINISH

1. At the start Cuban postman Felix Carvajal is wearing his smartest shirt, trousers and polished shoes. A few snips from some scissors quickly turn his trousers into shorts.

2. It's a very hot day. Horsemen gallop ahead raising so much dust that everybody starts choking. Neither the runners nor the cars following can see where they're going.

3. Two judges are hurt when their car crashes off the road.

4. South African Len Tau is chased miles off course by a large yellow dog.

Juicy apples. I'm starving.

5. Felix, in third place, stops to pick apples.

6. Fred Lotz of New York, USA gets cramps. He climbs into his trainer's car to drive back to the stadium.

7. Felix's apples were unripe!

Ow! Ow! My stomach aches.

This'll pep you up!

Thanks for the lift.

8. Thomas Hicks of Boston, USA is exhausted. His trainer gives him strychnine poison . . . to give him energy!

9. Fred's trainer's car breaks down. Fred decides to jog the last couple of miles back to the stadium.

10. Tom Hicks, stumbling along in a poisoned daze, is amazed when Fred races by, fresh as a daisy.

11. When Fred runs into the stadium, the crowds cheer. He's about to be given the gold medal when his cheating is revealed. Tom is declared champion although he's had to go straight to hospital. Only half the runners finish. Felix groans in at fourth. Len arrives ninth, having lost the dog.

It was only a joke.

AMSTERDAM

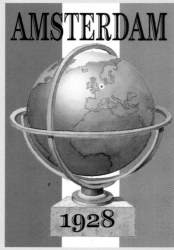

1928

Women's athletics finally introduced.

Swimming events for women had been going since 1912. In the 1928 breaststroke final, Hilde Schrader of Germany swam so fast that her swimsuit straps snapped. She was too shy to get out of the pool.

The longest of the new track events for women was the 800 metres. When several of the competitors lay down after the finish to get their breath back, the newspapers made up stories of how they'd collapsed during the race. This led to all future women's track events over 200 metres being banned.

LOS ANGELES

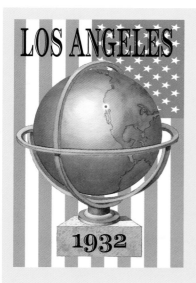

1932

The games were held in the LA Coliseum, the largest stadium in the world. One lonely athlete represented China. Sprinter Liu Chang Chun didn't win any medals but he did make history.

MIGHT'VE-BEEN WHO CAME BACK FROM THE DEAD

Betty Robinson

Betty of Chicago, USA won the first women's 100 metre gold in 1928. She missed the 1932 games because for seven months she'd been in a coma after a plane crash! But she recovered and came back to win a gold in the 1936 relay.

GREATEST ALL-ROUND MIGHT'VE-BEEN

Mildred 'Babe' Didrikson

Babe, from Texas, USA, was a champion at almost every sport. She broke records in javelin, hurdles, high-jump and baseball throw at the 1932 Amateur Championships. But in the Olympics she was only allowed to enter three events. She won two golds and a silver. Who knows how many more she might have won! Instead she turned pro at golf and won ten major championships.

WOMEN IN THE OLYMPICS

There were no female competitors in the ancient Games. Even in the modern era,
it took a long time before women were allowed to compete in more than a handful of events.

Women were not even allowed to attend the ancient Games at Olympia. Any caught sneaking in were taken to a nearby mountain and thrown off.

Rich women could enter chariot teams, as owners. The rest had to make do with the separate Games of Hera, consisting of just one foot race.

A Greek woman, Stamata Revithi, was so fed up at not being allowed to compete in the Marathon of 1896 that she ran the course by herself next day.

While visiting Paris in the summer of 1900 some women took part in sports such as ballooning, croquet and golf, not realising they were competing in the Games. Margaret Abbott of Chicago, USA won a golf tournament. She died in 1955 never knowing she'd been the first American woman to win gold.

Charlotte Cooper
UK tennis player – became first ever female gold in 1900.

MEN AND WOMEN COMPETE DIRECTLY

In sailing there have been mixed events since 1908 when Frances Rivett-Carnac, UK, became the first female gold crew-member.

In 1952 the equestrian events were opened to women and are today the only sport in which men and women compete one on one.

After 1928, the 800 metres for women was not run again until 1964! There was not even a female member of the IOC until 1984.

BERLIN

1936

First time the torch was carried from Olympia

DE COUBERTIN MEDAL
LUTZ LONG
for sportsmanship

Try it this way.

Thanks, Lutz.

The Nazis didn't allow any 'non-Aryan' Germans to compete. But not all Germans were racist. Lutz Long even advised Jesse Owens on his long-jump technique and, as a result, Jesse beat him.

The Games were televised for the first time. Unfortunately hardly anybody in those days had a TV set to watch them on.

US diver Marjorie Gestring (aged 13) became the youngest ever to win gold, Danish swimmer Inge Sorensen (aged 12) bronze.

THE MISSING OLYMPICS

The next Olympiad had been scheduled for Tokyo in 1940 but was cancelled when World War Two broke out. There were no more games until 1948.

LONDON

1948

He's too heavy.

How about shaving all his hair off?

Although quite chaotic — the scales used to weigh the boxers were inaccurate and the judges lost count when Emil Zátopek lapped nearly all his competitors — the 1948 Games cheered the world up after the war. See page 28 for more.

THE BERLIN CHAMPION

Jesse Owens
Jesse, from Cleveland USA, won four golds in sprint, long jump and relay. This really annoyed Adolf Hitler, who believed Europeans were better at everything than people of African descent. Afterwards Jesse turned pro, so, sadly, he was banned from ever competing in the Olympics again.

THE FLYING HOUSEWIFE

Fanny Blankers-Koen
Because of the war, this Dutch mother of two missed any chance for Olympic medals until 1948 when she won four golds — in sprinting, hurdling and relay. She was a brilliant all-rounder and might have won medals in high and long jump too if she'd been allowed to enter more events.

HELSINKI

1952

First time a team from the USSR competed.

Fritz Schwab and Bruno Junk

The race-walking rules stated that all disqualifications must be handed out during the race. In the final, Fritz (Switzerland) and Bruno (USSR) ran to the finish line before the judges could catch them.

THE CZECH LOCOMOTIVE

Emil Zátopek

Emil got his nickname from the wheezing sound he made as he ran. He trained after work, at night in all weathers, wearing army boots. He not only won gold and broke the world records in the 5,000 and 10,000 in Helsinki but also in the Marathon, which he'd never run before. He became a hero among the Czech people but was disgraced by the government for supporting democracy.

MELBOURNE

1956

The first Olympiad to be held in the Southern Hemisphere

18-year-old Vyacheslav Ivanov (USSR) won his first of three golds for single sculls. He was so excited he threw it in the air but forgot to catch it. The medal disappeared to the bottom of the lake.

ROME

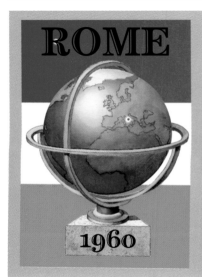

1960

Despite running barefoot and nearly colliding with a scooter, Abebe Bikila won the Marathon. Nobody expected an African to win. The band didn't even know the Ethiopian national anthem.

18-year-old boxer Cassius Clay from Kentucky, USA won light heavyweight gold. He changed his name in 1964... to Mohammed Ali.

MONTREAL

1976

Only host country to win no gold medals

> She only scored one!

> The scoreboard doesn't go up to ten.

Nadia Comaneci (Romania) took up gymnastics in kindergarten. In Montreal, aged 14, she was the first gymnast to score a ten and will always be youngest ever to win gold as competitors must now be sixteen.

TOP MALE GYMNAST

Sawao Kato

Sawao, from Nigata, Japan, won the first three of his eight golds in Mexico City and the last two in Montreal. This makes him the most successful male Olympic gymnast of all time.

MOSCOW

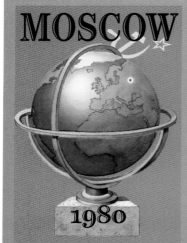

1980

The USA and sixty-four other countries did not send teams (see POLITICS page 23)

> Steve won the 800 metres.

> Seb won the 1,500.

Middle distance UK runners Sebastian Coe and Steve Ovett beat each other in the races they were expected to win. Lord Coe went on to take charge of organising London 2012.

NOT A KLUTZ
Paralysed By Fear

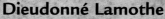

> You will run as though your life depends on it ... which it does!

Dieudonné Lamothe

Why was Dieudonné's 5000 metres in Montreal the slowest ever? Why did he trail in last in the Moscow Marathon? He explained years later. Baby Doc, the dictator of Haiti, had threatened him with death if he didn't finish. Instead of making him run faster, he was paralysed with fear. After Doc's overthrow, Dieudonné did much better, coming 20th in Seoul.

LOS ANGELES

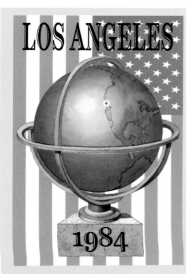

1984

Seventeen-year-old South African Zola Budd hero-worshipped world record holder Mary Decker (USA). But when she ran against Mary in the 3000 metre final, she accidentally tripped her.

SPORTSMAN OF THE CENTURY

Carl Lewis

In 1999 the IOC voted US sprinter Carl Lewis of Birmingham, Alabama, the twentieth century's greatest athlete. He won nine Olympic golds between 1984 and 1996, dominating the 100 metres, 200 metres and the long jump.

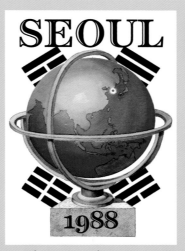

SEOUL

1988

The second games to be held in Asia

Korean Sohn Kee-Chung had annoyed Hitler as much as Jesse Owens had by winning the Berlin Marathon in 1936. Fifty-two years later, he carried the torch into the stadium in Seoul.

Christa Luding (Germany) won medals in both summer and winter Games of 1988 ... impossible now as these events are held two years apart.

EIGHT GOLDS SWIMMER

Matt Biondi

Matt, from California, USA, won a total of eight golds. He won five in Seoul, and broke four world records.

BARCELONA

1992

1992 saw big changes to some major medal-winning countries. The USSR was now split into fifteen separate nations while East and West Germany had been reunited.

Why's he not on video between start and finish?

KLUTZ ALERT!

How did he get there?

No sign of him after mile one.

Apolinario Gomez? My foot! That's Polin.

Polin Belisle

Despite doing mysteriously well in other Marathons, Polin came last in Seoul. Team Belize dropped him. Then in Barcelona his former teammates recognized a new Honduran runner. Even after Honduras dumped him, he still cheekily crashed the start ... and then he vanished.

ATLANTA

1996

Halfway through the Atlanta Games — one hundred years after the first modern Olympiad — a terrorist bomb exploded, killing one person and injuring over a hundred others. It was decided to continue the Games.

Hey! We forgot Kerri.

The hero of the games was 19-year-old gymnast Kerri Strug of Arizona, USA who vaulted with a badly sprained ankle to ensure her team won. She had to be carried onto the podium for the prize-giving and nearly got left behind when it was over.

SYDNEY

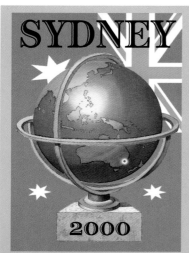

2000

This was only the second Olympiad to be held in the Southern hemisphere

You can do it.

KLUTZ ALERT!
Eric the Eel

Go Eric!

My muscles are aching.

Eric Moussambani
Eric of Equatorial Guinea had only just learnt to swim in a small hotel pool. His time was the slowest ever for the 100 metres, twice that of any of the other competitors … but his personal best!

LONGEST SERVING CHAMPION

Birgit Fischer
Kayaker Birgit of Brandenburg, Germany, won her first gold at Moscow in 1980 and her eighth twenty-four years later in Athens. With four silver medals as well, she is the second highest woman medal winner.

ATHENS

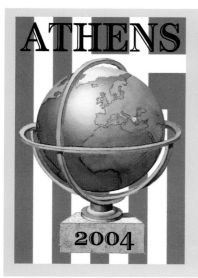

2004

The Olympic flame, first lit by the rays of the sun at a ceremony in ancient Olympia, was carried all around the world before returning to ignite the cauldron above the stadium in Athens.

BEIJING

2008

THE STADIUM nicknamed 'The Bird's Nest'. You can see why.

The games ended with spectacular fireworks, a 2000-year-old Chinese invention.

The biggest Games to date, with eleven thousand athletes from 204 countries. Huge amounts were spent on preparations, including the world's fastest train, biggest air terminal and the huge National Stadium. The opening ceremony had fifteen thousand performers. It began at 8.08 on the eighth day of the eighth month ... Eight is a very lucky number in China.

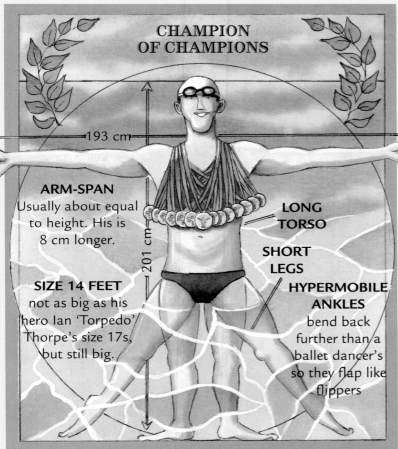

CHAMPION OF CHAMPIONS

193 cm

201 cm

ARM-SPAN
Usually about equal to height. His is 8 cm longer.

SIZE 14 FEET
not as big as his hero Ian 'Torpedo' Thorpe's size 17s, but still big.

LONG TORSO

SHORT LEGS

HYPERMOBILE ANKLES
bend back further than a ballet dancer's so they flap like flippers

Michael Phelps

After winning six golds in Athens, Michael, of Maryland, USA, won eight in Beijing, a total of fourteen ... more than any other Olympian ever! His body is perfect for swimming fast and not getting tired. As a child he was hyperactive but he's put all that activity to good use. In training, he eats 10,000 calories a day, five times more than an average man!

In 2004 the USA had led the gold medal table with thirty-six. China spent so much effort on training their athletes that in 2008 they topped the table with fifty-one. Among nine new events was Bicycle Motocross — BMX.

Two gold-winning Paralympians competed in the main games. Swimmer Natalie Du Toit of South Africa had lost her leg in a car accident. Table tennis player Natalya Partyka of Poland was born with no right arm.